JESU, JOY OF MAN'S DESIRING

CHORALE FROM CANTATA No. 147

J. S. BACH
Arranged for Piano by MYRA HESS

*   The notes in parentheses may be omitted.

**   Here and in similar passages the arranger plays this more correct version, which is to be preferred:

, The small notes are to be played, and are written thus to show the line of the melodic figure.

'Jesu, Joy of Man's Desiring' is the first line of an original poem by the late Robert Bridges and is used by permission.

This Chorale is also published in arrangements by Myra Hess for piano duet and for two pianos. Many other instrumental, orchestral, and choral arrangements are also available.

Cantando il soprano

3

Reproduced and printed by
Halstan & Co. Ltd., Amersham, Bucks., England

OXFORD UNIVERSITY PRESS